FIRST AMERICANS
The Lakota

MICHAEL BURGAN

Marshall Cavendish
Benchmark
New York

ACKNOWLEDGMENTS

Series consultant: Raymond Bial

Marshall Cavendish
99 White Plains Road
Tarrytown, New York 10591-5502
www.marshallcavendish.us

Text, maps, and illustrations copyright © 2009 by Marshall Cavendish Corporation
Map by Rodica Prato / Craft illustrations by Chris Santoro

Library of Congress Cataloging-in-Publication Data

Burgan, Michael.
The Lakota / by Michael Burgan.
p. cm. — (First Americans)
Summary: "Provides comprehensive information on the background, lifestyle,
beliefs, and present-day lives of the Lakota people"—Provided by publisher.
Includes bibliographical references and index.
ISBN 978-0-7614-3023-0
1. Teton Indians—History—Juvenile literature.   2. Teton Indians—Social
life and customs—Juvenile literature.   I. Title.
E99.T34B87 2007
978.004'9752—dc22
 2007035864

Front cover: A young Lakota Sioux boy, wearing a roach headdress, attends the Rosebud Powwow in South Dakota.
Title page: Detail of a Lakota Sioux tipi, painted with images of horses and buffalo
Photo research by: Connie Gardner
Cover photo by: Marilyn Angel Wynn/Native American Stock Photography
The photographs in this book are used by permission and through the courtesy of: *Native Stock:* Marilyn Angel Wynn, 1, 14, 22, 25, 29, 32, 34, 39; *Granger Collection:* 11; *The Image Works:* Andre Jenny, 4; Mary Evans Picture Library, 10, 19, Kent Meireis, 38; *NorthWind Picture Archives:* 6; *Corbis:* Laynne Kennedy, 8; *Getty Images:* Herbert Orth, 16; Mike Wolforth, 26.

Editor: Deborah Grahame
Publisher: Michelle Bisson
Art Director: Anahid Hamparian
Series Designer: Symon Chow

Printed in Malaysia
1 3 5 6 4 2

CONTENTS

1 · "FRIENDS" OF THE GREAT PLAINS

More than seven hundred years ago a Native American people lived in central Minnesota and parts of northern Wisconsin. The modern-day Indians who trace their roots to those people are known by many names. Most Americans call them the Sioux (SOO). The name comes from the Algonquian Indian phrase *Nadowe Su*, which means "little rattle." It refers to the rattle of a rattlesnake. French trappers later dropped the first word and spelled the second *Sioux*. The Sioux eventually split into smaller groups. The Sioux themselves say there were seven major groups, known as Seven Council Fires. One of the groups was the Lakota (Luh-KO-tuh). In their language this

The Lakota and other Sioux Indians once hunted on the open prairies of South Dakota. The area shown here is now part of the Sisseton Indian Reservation, home to the Sisseton-Wahpeton Sioux.

name means "an **alliance** of friends," or simply, "the friends." The Lakota are also sometimes called the Tetons.

Most likely the Sioux first settled in Minnesota after moving from lands farther south along the Mississippi River. In their new home the Sioux harvested wild rice that grew in lakes and streams. They also planted some corn, squash, and tobacco, and hunted deer and other forest animals for meat. The people built small villages near their farmlands,

In Minnesota, Sioux women went out once a year to harvest wild rice.

and sometimes erected tall, wooden fences around the villages to keep out enemies.

Over time the seven Sioux groups became three main groups, one of which was the Lakota. The other two major divisions were the Dakota (also called Santee) and the Yankton-Yanktonai (also called Nakota). Each of the three major groups were split into even smaller units called bands or tribes. The Lakota tribes included the Sicangu (Brulé), Oglala, Oohenonpa (Two Kettles), Sihasapa (Blackfeet), Minneconjou, Itazipco (Sans Arc), and Hunkpapa.

By the 1600s the Sioux, including the Lakota, were moving westward as other Indian tribes pushed into Minnesota seeking hunting grounds. The Sioux began to settle on the grass-covered prairie of what are now northern Iowa and North and South Dakota. By the end of the 1700s the Lakota were living farthest west of the three groups, having crossed the Missouri River and entered the northern **Great Plains**. The Oglala were often pioneers, heading into new lands before the other Lakota bands. They settled in the Black Hills of western South Dakota, which became a center of Lakota life.

The Great Plains stretch between the Mississippi River and the Rocky Mountains, and from southern Canada to northern Texas. Although this area is mostly flat and covered with grass, it also has rolling hills and some woodland along its rivers. The Great Plains was also home to millions of bison, or buffalo. The large, shaggy animals roamed the plains eating grass and sometimes berries.

The buffalo was an important part of life for the Lakota and other Indians of the Great Plains. The animal was a major

A male bison, or buffalo, can stand up to six feet tall at the shoulder and weigh almost one ton.

source of food, and almost every part of its body was useful in some way. The Lakota turned buffalo hides into robes and other clothing. They made tools from buffalo bones and thread from **sinew**. They also used the dried hide to cover tipis, their cone-shaped homes. Held up by poles, tipis were easy to set up and take down. This was crucial to the Lakota, who moved often to follow buffalo herds and other game.

Although the Europeans brought guns and other goods that the Lakota valued, their presence became a threat to all the Sioux and their neighbors. The Lakota had never been exposed to smallpox and other diseases that the Europeans carried to North America. These diseases were deadly to the Indians because their bodies did not have natural defenses to fight them. **Epidemics** of smallpox killed some Brulé Lakota in the early 1780s and during 1801–1802. But because the Lakota were always on the move, they did not suffer as much as the tribes that stayed in one place.

By the late 1700s English colonists had won their independence and established the United States of America. In

Using rifles made it easier for the Lakota to hunt buffalo. The tribes traded for the guns with American settlers and other Native Americans.

1803 the U.S. government bought a huge piece of land from France. The territory stretched west of the Mississippi River but also included New Orleans and the eastern part of Louisiana state. Called the Louisiana Purchase, it included the new homeland of the Lakota Sioux. The next year Meriwether Lewis and William Clark led the first U.S. **expedition** into Lakota lands. The explorers wanted to build good relations with the native people who now occupied large parts of the northern Great Plains. Instead, the first meeting with the Lakota almost led to violence. Relations improved a bit in 1825, when the Lakota signed a treaty of trade and friendship with the U.S. government.

In the decades that followed, U.S. settlers headed west. Many were drawn by the discovery of gold in California in

Meriwether Lewis (with rounded hat) and William Clark (to his right) met with Brulé Lakota and other Sioux Indians during their travels in South Dakota.

1848. Once again they brought diseases that killed some Lakota. In 1851, hoping to keep relations peaceful, the U.S. government called a meeting with the Great Plains Indians at Fort Laramie, Wyoming. The Lakota and other tribes agreed not to attack trading posts and to live only in certain areas. In return the Americans promised to give the Indians goods worth $50,000 every year for fifty years.

The treaty did not keep the peace, however. In 1854 some Brulé Lakota killed a cow that belonged to settlers in Utah. This and other minor incidents led U.S troops to attack the Lakota, and a major battle was fought. Conflicts erupted again through the 1860s and 1870s, especially after American settlers discovered gold in the Black Hills in Dakota territory. The Lakota and their **allies** tried to stop the settlers from moving onto their lands, because the settlers began to slaughter the buffalo herds the Indians needed to survive. Crazy Horse and Red Cloud of the Oglala, and Sitting Bull, a Hunkpapa, were important chiefs who led the Lakota during these conflicts.

In 1866 Red Cloud led attacks on U.S. troops in Wyoming, and he later forced the American soldiers to leave forts in the region. U.S. officials signed a peace treaty in 1868, then began to make plans to force the Lakota onto **reservations** in western South Dakota. Red Cloud said he was tricked, because the U.S. government claimed that he had agreed to send his people to reservations. Oglala and other Lakota did not want to go to the reservations. They were especially angry when, in 1874, Lieutenant Colonel George Custer made plans to build a fort in the Black Hills, which were sacred, or holy, to the Lakota.

In June 1876 about two thousand Lakota and their allies fought U.S. soldiers at the Little Bighorn River in eastern Montana. Led by Crazy Horse and Sitting Bull, the Lakota won a major victory, killing Custer and more than two hundred of his men. But even with this victory the Lakota could not stop the U.S. government from taking over their traditional lands.

Some Lakota tried to resist, but most accepted that they

Crazy Horse

Crazy Horse has been called the greatest Lakota war leader. He was born around 1840 and nicknamed Curly Hair. His father, also named Crazy Horse, was an Oglala chief. His mother came from the Minneconjou band. From an early age Crazy Horse believed the Lakota should resist American efforts to limit their freedom. In 1876 he fought at the Battle of the Little Big Horn, one of the Indians' greatest victories against the U.S. Army. Before the battle he showed his fearless nature. He shouted to his warriors, "Come on, Lakotas! It's a good day to die." Crazy Horse won great fame for his bravery during the battle. In 1877, however, Crazy Horse and his men had run out of food and were tired of war. The chief gave himself up to U.S. officials. After four months on the reservation in Nebraska, he left without permission, and was arrested. At first he did not resist, but he struggled when he thought he was being sent to jail. He was killed by a U.S. soldier. Today Crazy Horse is honored for his efforts to preserve the Lakota way of life.

Crazy Horse (ca. 1840–1877) joined his first war party when he was just twelve years old.

would have to live on the reservations. Sitting Bull fled to Canada for a time, but later turned himself in and lived on Standing Rock Reservation in the Dakota Territory. He briefly appeared in "Wild West" shows created by William "Buffalo Bill" Cody. Some Lakota found comfort in a new spiritual movement called the Ghost Dance, which started in Nevada and spread to the Black Hills. Believers thought special dances could help bring back the old Indian ways. U.S. officials feared that the dancers were actually part of preparations for a new war against the Americans.

Sitting Bull did not take part in the Ghost Dance, but the Americans feared he would stir up feelings against them. On December 15, 1890, he was killed by Lakota police sent by the U.S. government to arrest him. Two weeks later, the Americans killed about two hundred Minneconjou Lakota Ghost Dancers at Wounded Knee, South Dakota. This **massacre** has been called the last major battle between U.S. troops and Native Americans. After the battle the Lakota had to accept life on the reservation.

2 · LAKOTA WAYS OF LIFE

When they set up camp Lakota bands placed their tipis in a circle. One large tipi near the entrance served as a "town hall," where the camp's men met to make rules for all camp members to follow. Sometimes women were allowed to speak at these meetings, but in general, men made the rules for the camp. Men called *akicita* acted like sheriffs. They made sure everyone followed the camp's rules. If a man did not like the rules of a camp, he could move his family's tipi outside of the circle and try to form his own camp, if friends and relatives chose to join him.

Within a camp the men worked together to track and kill buffalo. The men also carried out raids on enemy tribes. The Lakota were expert horse riders and fighters who were known

George Catlin, a famous artist of the nineteenth century, painted many scenes of Native American life. This work shows a Sioux camp, with several tipis.

across the Great Plains for their skills. The Lakota did not fight to take control of other tribes' lands. Most often the warriors' goal was to steal horses and prove their bravery. At times they might also fight to take revenge for an enemy's raids on them.

For the Lakota, **counting coup** was the greatest sign of a warrior's skill. This involved riding close to an enemy warrior and touching him with a stick. Each time a Lakota counted coup or performed another act of bravery, he received a feather. Warriors wore these feathers in headdresses so everyone could easily see their skills as a fighter.

Lakota men had a number of warrior societies that they could join. Each society had its own songs and dances that members performed at their meetings. One society, called the Kit Foxes, was for warriors who showed great bravery. A man had to be asked to join the Kit Fox society. Another society was called the Brave Hearts. They promised to help women, children, and the weak if they faced danger, especially during wartime. Only chiefs were allowed to join the Silent Eaters

Lakota hunters rest. They might cover up to twenty-five miles in one day while tracking buffalo.

society. The members were called Silent Eaters because they never spoke when they ate at festivals. Silent Eaters were elder males who had been warriors but were now too old to fight with war parties. They had the right to speak at meetings any time they wished.

For Lakota women, life centered around the home. A wife owned the family's tipi and was in charge of setting it up.

Build a Model Shield

On their shields Lakota warriors painted sacred images that they believed would protect them in battle. This fun activity will show you how to build a model of a shield.

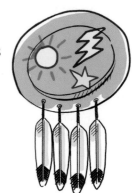

You will need:

- A large, sturdy paper or plastic plate
- A piece of cardboard, longer than the plate's width
- 3 or 4 feathers from a craft store
- Markers or paint
- One-hole punch

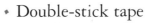

- Double-stick tape
- 3 or 4 pieces of thread or string, about 16 inches long (40.5 centimeters)

What you do:

1· On the bottom side of the plate draw or paint a picture of a favorite animal or a scene from nature.

2· Cut a strip of cardboard 1 inch (2.5 cm) wide and 1 inch (2.5 cm) longer than the width of the plate. Staple each end of the cardboard strip along the edge of the middle of the plate's front (the side you didn't draw on). The strip should form the shape of a bow used with a bow and arrow.*

3· Along the bottom edge of the plate, punch 1 hole for each feather you have. Space the holes about an inch or so apart.

4· Wrap a piece of double-stick tape around the shaft of each feather.

5· Wrap 1 piece of string over the tape, starting from the edge of the shaft closest to the feather. Cover all of the tape with the string. Do this with each feather.

6· Tie the end of the thread on each feather through the holes in the bottom of the plate.

*Use the stapled strip to hold the shield or to display it on a wall.

This dress and other Lakota clothing was made from buffalo hide.

The wife was also in charge of taking the tipi down. The women gathered nuts, wild berries, and vegetables, and sometimes raised small amounts of corn. However, most corn, as well as squash and beans, came from trading with other tribes.

Another important chore for women was skinning and cutting up buffalo after they were killed. The meat was divided among all the families of the camp. Thin strips of meat were dried to make **jerky**, which could be stored for months. Some of the jerky was mixed with chokecherries or other berries to create **pemmican**. This dried food could last for several years. The wife of the warrior who killed the buffalo received the hide, which was

A Sioux Soup

The Lakota and other Sioux ate wild turnips that grew across the Great Plains. The recipe below would normally be made with buffalo bones, but beef can be used instead. Make sure to have an adult help you in the kitchen.

What you need:

- 1 1/2 pounds meaty beef bones
- 6 cups beef broth or water
- Salt and pepper to taste
- 1 cup fresh or frozen corn
- 2 cups diced turnip or 3/4 cup diced turnip, 1/2 cup diced rutabaga, and 1 diced parsnip

What you do:

1. Place all the ingredients in a pot except the salt and pepper.
2. Bring the broth or water to a boil.
3. Reduce the heat to a simmer.
4. Skim off any foam that rises to the surface of the pot.
5. Cover and cook the soup for 30 to 60 minutes.
6. Remove the bones from the soup. After they have cooled, remove the meat from the bones and return the meat to the soup.
7. Season with salt and pepper.

tanned so it could be made into clothing. Deer and elk skins were also used to make clothes.

Women took care of the children when they were young. When a boy's voice began to deepen, usually around age twelve or thirteen, he went off with his father and the other men of the camp to learn the skills of a warrior. Younger boys, along with girls, helped the women of the camp gather firewood and collect wild berries and nuts. As the girls got older they learned how to skin buffalo, sew, and set up tipis. For fun Lakota children played with tops, and they also played a game that used small "bowling balls" made of stones.

Lakota children learned about the tribe's history, beliefs, and practices in several ways. Each camp had at least one storyteller who recited the tribe's stories. Children also learned from all the adults around them. The Lakota also recorded their history using drawings. These drawings were called winter counts. The Lakota marked one year as the time between one winter's first snow and the next winter's. The winter count served as the tribe's calendar and history book.

The drawings in a winter count marked important events in a tribe's history.

To the Lakota the entire universe was the creation of *Wakan Tanka*, the Great (or Holy) Spirit. Some Lakota said that *Wakan Tanka* had a male side, called *Tunkashila*, and female side, which was the earth. All people, animals, and plants are connected through *Wakan Tanka*. Even rocks and other non-living things are related to living things, because they all come from the Creator.

In their daily lives the Lakota honored *Wakan Tanka* and other holy spirits and items. Some of the spirits helped humans, while others could be evil. The most important item to the Lakota was the *Chanunpa*, or sacred pipe. They believed that the first pipe had been brought to them by White Buffalo Calf Woman, a holy being who later turned into

A huge statue honoring Crazy Horse is being carved in the Black Hills. The Lakota believed that spirits called Thunder Beings blessed him.

a buffalo and then disappeared. At all their sacred ceremonies the Lakota smoked the pipe. They believed the smoke brought something *wakan* (holy) to the smokers. When the smokers exhaled, the smoke carried their requests to *Wakan Tanka*.

When they smoked the pipe the Lakota offered praise to the four directions: east, west, north, and south. Each direction had a special color and its own wind, which had certain powers. These were represented on a circle with a cross over it, called a medicine wheel. The earth, sun, moon, and stars were other powerful spirits that the Lakota honored, along with water, fire, and air.

The Lakota also believed that animals were sacred. The most important animal was the buffalo. They considered it a generous creature that gave up its own life so the Lakota could survive. Drawings of buffalos or real buffalo skulls were used in many ceremonies. The eagle also played a special role in Lakota spiritual life. It represented strength, and served as a messenger between the Lakota and *Wakan Tanka*.

Like many tribes, the Lakota had skilled spiritual leaders called medicine men or **shamans**. They were born with an understanding of everything *wakan*, although they had to go through special training to develop their skills. Shamans

A large medicine wheel made of rocks painted yellow, red, white, and black. Each of the four directions is associated with a color, though different tribes use different colors for each direction.

taught other Lakota about the tribe's spiritual ways and helped them understand what the spirits wanted them to do. Shamans also served as healers. The Lakota believed that, through their contact with the spirit world, the shamans could cure the sick. Shamans often used herbal teas and roots as medicine.

The Lakota had seven major spiritual rites and ceremonies. They believed that White Buffalo Calf Woman gave them these rites. The rites include the ceremony for two people to form a special bond called *Hunka*, the rite that marks a girl's becoming an adult woman, and the use of the *Inipi*, or sweat lodge. Inside a dome-shaped hut, hot rocks raise the temperature. Sweating is believed to remove evil spirits and to prepare a Lakota to receive messages from *Wakan Tanka*.

The Lakota entered the sweat lodge before heading out for another of the seven rites, the vision quest. Men, and sometimes women, used the vision quest as a way to contact the spirits. Before the quest they talked with a shaman, who offered them guidance on what to do. Then the person seeking knowledge headed out alone into the wilderness for up to four days. He or she took only a pipe and some tobacco to help him or her contact the spirit world. When seekers returned they explained to the shaman the vision that filled their minds while they were away. He helped them understand what it meant and how they should use that knowledge in their daily life.

The throwing of the ball, or *Tapa Wankaye Yapi*, was a ceremony in which a young girl, representing purity, threw a ball made of buffalo skin and hide in the four directions: east, west, north, and south. As the ball returned to earth, the power of *Wankan Tanka* came down upon the Lakota people.

The most important of the seven Lakota **rituals** was the Sun Dance. This ceremony was common during the nineteenth century, and is sometimes still practiced today, although its form has changed. The traditional Sun Dance lasted for four days. The main dancers who took part, usually men, offered their thanks to the spirits for helping them. Other times the dancers asked the spirits for help with something they planned to do.

A special site was chosen for the Sun Dance, and a pole made from a cottonwood tree was placed in the center. The ceremony included singing and dancing. On the last day

The Sun Dance could be performed to offer thanks for spiritual help already received, as well as to ask for help in future events.

the main dancers had their chest skin pierced and a bone passed through the openings. The bone was then attached to leather ropes, which were tied to the center pole. The dancers then moved about, trying to remove the bones from their chest. The pain of the dance was meant to show the spirits that the dancers were worthy of help. The scars left from this ritual told all other Lakota of the dancers' bravery and sacrifice. No one ever doubted the word of a person who wore those scars.

The last ritual for any Lakota was the keeping of the soul. The Lakota believed that when people died, their souls left their bodies and rose up to *Wakan Tanka*. To prepare for this trip the soul had to be cleansed. This involved burning sweetgrass near a lock of the dead person's hair. The hair was then placed in a piece of buffalo skin and kept by a relative for one year. After a year the skin was opened, and the dead person's soul was believed to go to *Wakan Tanka*. Bodies of the deceased were placed on burial **scaffolds** or in the branches of a tree.

4 · THE LAKOTA TODAY

The Wounded Knee Massacre of 1890 marked the end of the old way of life for the Lakota. Even before then, some tribal members had given up their nomadic ways and settled on one of five reservations in South Dakota. The U.S. government wanted the Lakota to become farmers, but few of them had the money they needed to raise enough crops to sell. Some Lakota rented their land to settlers and, after 1887, the U.S. government allowed the settlers to buy some of it.

Missionaries tried to **convert** the Lakota to Christianity, and the U.S. government forbade the Sun Dance. Some Lakota secretly practiced their rituals, however, so the traditional beliefs never died out. But the members who cut their hair and wore American-style clothing were more likely to get

This building serves as the tribal office for the Lakota who live on the Standing Rock Reservation, which includes land in both North and South Dakota.

jobs working for the government. Some Lakota children were forced to go to schools off the reservation. They learned to read and write in English, which could help them get jobs when they were older. But the schools also denied them the chance to learn traditional Lakota ways.

The U.S. government gave the Lakota and other Sioux money and food to help them survive. This help, however, was small, and the Lakota lived in deep poverty. Some Lakota, both men and women, looked for jobs off the reservations. Men might work in construction, while the women often took jobs working as housekeepers for non-Indian families. In most cases the Lakota struggled to make enough money to live.

Life on the reservations was especially hard during the Great Depression of the 1930s. Across the United States millions of people lost jobs and struggled to survive. A terrible **drought** also gripped much of the Great Plains. South Dakota farmers saw their crops fail, and many tribal members almost starved. But during these years the U.S. government gave the tribes money to try to develop new businesses. The Indian Reorganization Act of 1934 also gave the Lakota and other tribes greater freedom to pursue their old culture and govern themselves as they chose.

After the United States entered World War II in 1941, about 25,000 Native American men and women volunteered for the military. A few Lakota served as "code talkers" and sent and received top-secret messages that were translated from English into the Lakota language. No enemy soldiers knew the Lakota language, so they could not figure out the messages. Tens of thousands of tribal members also left the reservations to take jobs in cities, a practice that continued after the war.

During their decades on the reservations the Lakota fought legal and political battles to try to regain some of what they had lost. In 1911 some of them formed the Black Hills Treaty Council to try to win back control of the Black Hills, which the Lakota consider sacred. The effort failed. In 1944 Charles Heacock, from the Rosebud Sioux Reservation,

In the 2000s, Russell Means led protests against Columbus Day, saying the coming of Europeans to North America brought great suffering to Native Americans.

helped form the National Congress of American Indians. The congress wanted all Indian nations to work together to protect the rights that were given to them in old treaties with the U.S. government. During the late 1960s Russell Means, an Oglala Lakota, became a leader of the American Indian Movement (AIM). Its members protested the continuing poverty and unequal legal treatment that many tribes faced.

In 1973 Means was one of several AIM members who went to Wounded Knee to protest conditions on the reservations. A gun battle erupted between the Indians and U.S. officials. This second Wounded Knee incident brought new attention to the problems the Lakota faced. It also led some younger tribal members to explore their native language and culture.

This museum in Wall, South Dakota, explains the details of the Wounded Knee Massacre of 1890. Today, tourists often visit the Lakota reservations and nearby sites important to their history.

In 1980 the U.S. government took one step to help the Lakota. A U.S. court gave the Lakota $105 million as payment for their loss of the Black Hills. The tribe, however, refused the money, because they still wanted the land, which they considered their traditional homeland.

Today more Lakota are starting small businesses. Tourism is a major source of income for the Lakota. Visitors pay entrance fees to explore the land's natural beauty and museums that describe Sioux history. Some reservations also offer gambling.

LAKOTA

NORTH DAKOTA

MONTANA

STANDING ROCK
RESERVATION

CHEYENNE RIVER
RESERVATION

WYOMING

SOUTH DAKOTA

LOWER BRULE
RESERVATION

PINE RIDGE
RESERVATION

MISSOURI RIVER

ROSEBUD
RESERVATION

NEBRASKA

This map shows the five Lakota reservations. Four more in the eastern part of South Dakota are home to other Sioux tribes.

The Lakota Reservations of South Dakota

Name	Tribal Members	Bands
Cheyenne River	12,000	Minneconjou Sans Arc Blackfeet Two Kettle
Lower Brulé	2,500	Brulé
Standing Rock	10,859*	Hunkpapa Blackfeet
Rosebud	15,438	Brulé
Pine Ridge	17,775	Oglala

* Includes other Sioux

Life is still difficult for the Lakota. Certain illnesses, such as diabetes and alcoholism, pose many health problems. Some tribal members still struggle to make money. But the Lakota are continuing to bring back their old way of life. The Lakota language is taught in schools, and shamans practice many of the old rituals. The Lakota take pride in their history and look forward to a better future.

· TIME LINE

The Spanish bring horses to North America.

The Lakota move out of Minnesota and into South Dakota.

The Lakota obtain their first horses.

U.S. explorers Lewis and Clark meet the Lakota.

The U.S. government and the Lakota sign a treaty of friendship.

The Lakota join other Great Plains tribes in signing a treaty with the United States.

Red Cloud leads attacks on U.S. troops in Wyoming.

1519   1600s   Early 1700s   1803   1825   1851   1866

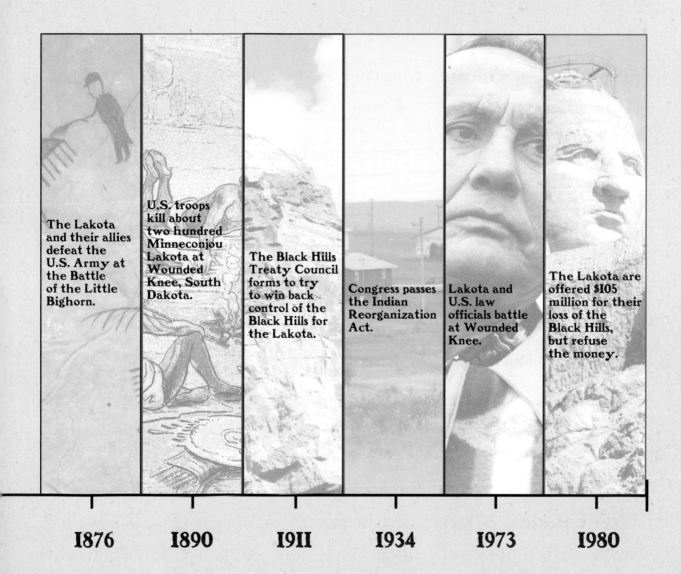

The Lakota and their allies defeat the U.S. Army at the Battle of the Little Bighorn.

U.S. troops kill about two hundred Minneconjou Lakota at Wounded Knee, South Dakota.

The Black Hills Treaty Council forms to try to win back control of the Black Hills for the Lakota.

Congress passes the Indian Reorganization Act.

Lakota and U.S. law officials battle at Wounded Knee.

The Lakota are offered $105 million for their loss of the Black Hills, but refuse the money.

1876   1890   1911   1934   1973   1980

· GLOSSARY

alliance: The joining together of people or nations to meet common goals.

allies: People or nations who work together to fight a common enemy.

convert: To cause someone to change his or her beliefs.

counting coup: Touching an enemy with one's hand or a stick, then getting away unharmed.

drought: A long period without rain.

epidemics: Wide outbreaks of deadly diseases.

expedition: A long journey made to explore lands or carry out trade.

Great Plains: A large area of North America that is covered with different kinds of grasses and stretches between the

Mississippi River and the Rocky Mountains, and from southern Canada to northern Texas.

jerky: Strips of dried meat.

massacre: The brutal killing of large numbers of people, who often don't have a way to defend themselves.

pemmican: Dried meat that is pounded into a powder and mixed with berries and animal fat.

reservations: Lands set aside for Native Americans to live on, after they gave up their claim to lands where they used to live.

rituals: Acts performed in a precise way at special ceremonies.

scaffold: A platform set above ground level.

shamans: Another name for medicine men, the healers and spiritual leaders of many Native American tribes.

sinew: A strong band of tissue that connects a muscle to a bone.

• FIND OUT MORE

Books

Patent, Dorothy Hinshaw. *The Buffalo and the Indian: A Shared Destiny.* New York: Clarion Books, 2006.

Todd, Anne M. *Crazy Horse, 1842–1877.* Mankato, MN: Blue Earth Books, 2003.

Trumbauer, Lisa. *Sitting Bull.* Mankato, MN: Capstone Press, 2004.

Yacowitz, Caryn. *Lakota Indians.* Chicago: Heinemann Library, 2003.

Web Sites

Crazy Horse Memorial
http://www.crazyhorse.org

Lakota Winter Counts
http://wintercounts.si.edu

Red Cloud Indian School
http://www.redcloudschool.org

About the Author

Michael Burgan is a former editor at Weekly Reader, where he wrote about current events. As a freelance author, he has written more than 150 books for children and young adults, mostly nonfiction. He is also a playwright. Burgan has a B.A. in history from the University of Connecticut, and currently resides with his wife in Chicago.

· INDEX

Page numbers in **boldface** are illustrations.